Div ye myn Lang Tam?

An Oral History of Robert Gordon's College

– based on the recollections of former pupils

Compiled by Philip Skingley
Robert Gordon's College

Published by – Robert Gordon's College
Schoolhill
Aberdeen
AB10 1FE

Published – 2000

ISBN – 0-9538807-0-2

Printed by – Compass Print
Hareness Road
Altens Industrial Estate
Aberdeen
AB12 3LE

Pupils past and present who have contributed to this project either as interviewers or interviewees -

Edgar Allan (1930 – 42)
John Anderson (1925 – 34)
Gordon Arthur (1940 – 45)
Eric Auld (1943 – 48)
Charles Benzies (1960 – 73)
Charles Bisset (1931 – 37)
Jennifer Black (1990 – 95)
William Brown (1926 – 32)
Robert Bruce (1934 – 40)
Robert Chisholm (1962 – 66)
David Christie (1992 – 98)
John Croll (1926 – 36)
John Cruickshank (1926 – 32)
Douglas Davidson (1944 – 50)
Lynn Davies (1992 – 98)
Ken Eddie (1947– 58)
Dr John Edward (1952 – 58)
Ian Elder (1937 – 42)
Niall Farquharson (1971 – 77)
Gordon Fergus (1981 – 87)
James Ferguson (1970 – 78)
Bruce Finlayson (1944 – 50)
Russell Fraser (1992 – 98)
Nicol Geddes (1948 – 57)
Jennifer Graham (1991 – 95)
Alexander Gray (1912 – 13)
W. D. "Buff" Hardie (1943 – 49)
Gillian Hekelaar (1992 – 98)
Dr Ian Hunter (1945 – 48)
Iain Hustwick (1932 – 41)
Robert Hutcheson (1990 – 98)
Alan Innes (1949 – 62)
Colin Johnston (1961 – 67)
Alan Kennedy (1938 – 41)
Andrew Kostulin (1961 – 68)
Esther Krukowski (1989 – 95)
Sandy Lunan (1953 – 58)
Arthur McCombie (1940 – 46)
Scott McKenzie (1975 – 88)
Alan McLean (1974 – 80)
Ronald McLeod (1929 – 35)
Melanie Marshall (1992 – 98)
Charles Milne (1936 – 42)
Craig Milne (1985 – 98)
David Milne (1951 – 62)
Ian Morrice (1942 – 54)
Ramsay Mowat (1947 – 58)
Duncan Munro (1960 – 69)
Andrew Paterson (1991 – 97)
Keith Philip (1955 – 61)
John Reid (1930 – 36)
Colin Runcie (1970 – 78)
Graham Sangster (1964 – 72)
Kenneth Scott (1992 – 98)
Alistair Simpson (1991 – 97)
William Sinclair (1924 – 27)
Howard Smith (1949 – 60)
John Souter (1940 – 51)
Ian Spence (1941 – 51)
Joseph Stead (1985 – 98)
(W.R.) Ron Steel (1975 – 78)
Elizabeth Templeton (1990 – 94)
Alan Towns (1960 – 66)
William Turbet (1990 – 98)
Michael Watson (1962 – 68)
George Wilson (1937 – 40)
Stephen Witte (1985 – 98)
Sarah Wyatt (1989
Forbes Young (1952 – 57)

Those who have helped in other ways to produce this history –

John Reid – proof reading
Ann Gannon and Pamela Cowling – searching out Gordonians
General Office Staff (Nora Smith, Sandra Fraser, Fiona McKay)
John Dow – proof reading
John Gordon and Arthur McCombie – contacting Gordonians / proof reading
Ken Morrice – poem
Elaine Brazendale and Penny Hartley – photographs / Gordonian Magazines
Rod Richmond – photographs
Bob Leggate – catering for group interviews
Brian Lockhart – press cuttings / proof reading
Iain McKenzie – diaries
Rhonda McColgan – school song
Tom Cumming – tape recorders
Donald Murray, Andrew Bell and Andrew Sivel – art work
George Barton – proof reading
Iain Davidson – conducting interviews
June Allan – transcribing
Bob Duncan – photographs / proof reading
Howard Smith – contacting Gordonians / photographs
Urwin Woodman – proof reading

Introduction / disclaimer !

With the approach of the Millennium and, coincidentally, the 250th anniversary of the opening of Robert Gordon's Hospital, it was felt appropriate that a history of the College be compiled based on the oral recollections of former pupils. Initially it was hoped that this could be based on individual interviews conducted by pupils in the senior part of the school. Accordingly, under the guidance of Dr. Iain Davidson (a Gordon's pupil between 1944 and 1950), S6 volunteers were given some basic training and began interviewing Gordonians in the autumn of 1996. The interviews were tape recorded and then transcribed by the young interviewers. These transcriptions provided much interesting and invaluable material going back to the 1920's, but the process - despite the enthusiasm of the pupils - proved very slow and time consuming. The decision was then made, in order to involve more Gordonians and to speed the process up, to conduct "group" interviews. With the help of John Gordon (1944-50) and Arthur McCombie (1940-46) a group of pupils from the 1930's was contacted and invited to come to the College. We assumed, rightly as it turned out, that the offer of a free lunch would be irresistible to a Gordonian and this first group duly assembled on Thursday 26 March 1998 !

The 1930's Group

Back Row - Philip Skingley, Andrew Christie (1992-98), Robert Hutcheson (1990-98), Kenneth Scott (1992-98), Brian Lockhart
Middle Row - Iain Davidson (1944-50), Charles Bisset (1931-37), John Croll (1926-36), Lynn Davies (1992-98), Gillian Hekelaar (1992-98)
Front Row - Robert Bruce (1934-40), Ronald McLeod (1929-35), William Brown (1926-32), John Reid (1930-36)

After recording this very successful interview it was decided to continue with this format and interview groups of pupils from each decade, up to and including the 1990's.

The text for this short "history" is therefore based almost entirely on the memories and recollections of Gordonians who kindly agreed to be interviewed between 1996 and 2000. Some information is derived from other sources most notably *"The Gordonian"* from where a number of photographs and illustrations have been reproduced. This work is not intended to be a definitive history of Gordon's in the twentieth century - even although the oral evidence covers most of the last century of the Millennium. Unsurprisingly these recollections and anecdotes tend to be highly selective and highly personalised, reflecting not the big educational issues of those days but much more the characters and incidents which colour so much of what they tell us were the happiest days of our lives. Although the tapes and transcripts record many fond memories, it has to be said that for some interviewees Gordon's of old was not a happy environment. It would be unfair to these contributors to pretend otherwise. In sharp contrast to today, Gordon's proved a less than sympathetic environment for those less academically able and who could not compensate for this by being good at sport. Thus it is hoped that a balanced representation of the views of ex-pupils has been achieved.

A great many people have been involved in producing this oral history. A list of those many and varied contributors is included and I would like to express my gratitude to them. I would like to offer particular thanks to Dr. Iain Davidson for his help in the planning and interviewing processes; and also Mrs.June Allan who willingly agreed to transcribe several of the group and individual interview tapes at a time when progress on this front was unavoidably delayed.

Although over seventy ex-pupils have been interviewed as part of this project, they do represent a very limited cross section of the Gordonian population. Furthermore the focus of attention has almost entirely been on the senior school. Consequently there will be aspects of school life and pupil activities - particularly at the junior school level - which will not be covered and which many would deem significant. Similarly there will be many worthy members of staff who have not been referred to. I apologise in advance for any such omissions. Finally therefore I would like to dedicate this oral history to all the many pupils and staff who, over the years, have worked tirelessly and given great service to the College but are not mentioned here.

P.J.S April 2000

Chapter 1

Bursaries, Foundations and Scholarships

It is perhaps appropriate to begin an "oral" history of Gordon's College by looking at some of the comments and recollections regarding bursaries, foundations and scholarships. It was the intention of Robert Gordon to provide an education for boys who, at that time , would not have been able to receive it. An extract from his Deed of Mortification and Disposition indicates Gordon's desire to provide

> *".....the building of an Hospital, and for Maintenance, Aliment, Entertainment, and Education of young Boys, whose parents are poor and indigent, and not able to maintain them at Schools, and put them to Trades and Employment."*

The building of Gordon's Hospital was not unique in eighteenth century Scotland and similar institutions existed , for example in Edinburgh, thanks to the benevolence of George Heriot and George Watson. However by the twentieth century many hundreds of boys in the north east of Scotland had benefited from Gordon's desire to provide an education for the sons of the less well off. Indeed as the last century progressed there continued to be much evidence of the advantages offered by the bursary / foundation system.

Like many others William *"Smiler"* Sinclair (1924-27) received a bursary and also like many others, would not have been able to attend Gordon's College without it. According to Bill Brown (1926-32),

> *"Foundationers got £14 per year and fees cancelled".*

Charles Bisset (1931-37) informs us that

> *"A bursary was £12 per year and fees paid and we could go to 352 King Street, the Endowments Trust, to collect 10 shillings, which helped us with books".*

Not surprisingly competition for such awards was fierce. George Wilson (1937-40) records that

> *"....while I was at Ferryhill Primary School I was encouraged to sit the exam. for a bursary to attend Robert Gordon's College when I was twelve years old. Around 200 pupils of my age attended the examination".*

As a result of this a Foundation was awarded

".....which paid my fees at the College and I received a sum of £36 spread over three years to pay for books, etc".

John Edward (1952-58) who became School Captain and is remembered by his contemporaries as a great all-round sportsman, gives some indication of the advantages which Gordon's was able to offer,

".....it was the greatest thing that ever happened to me, coming here, having come from Torry Junior Secondary....it was a relief to get here !".

In addition to bursary and foundation awards, the College has been able to offer financial support from other sources. A number of pupils from the 1930's and 1940's have referred to the Peter Scatterty Scholarships. The minutes of one of the Governors' meetings for 1936 record that,

"In 1936 Peter Scatterty of Johannesburg, a native of Aberdeenshire bequeathed to Robert Gordon's College a sum of £47,000. The Governors have decided to donate part of the annual revenue from the bequest to provide scholarships...."

The merits of the awards system have been commented on in a very positive way by almost all contributors. One of the 1970's group said,

" The bursary system was a good system. Looking back you mixed with a variety of children from different backgrounds. We didn't come from particularly wealthy backgrounds".

For Gordon Fergus (1981-87) the fees paid by Aberdeen Endowment Trust meant that he was able to attend the College and this would have been out of the question without such financial support.

One would expect the bursary/foundation/scholarship system to have created divisions among the pupils by engendering a sense of resentment or superiority among the fee paying pupils. The responses from former pupils on this issue strongly suggests that this was far from being the case. The 1930's group agreed that financial arrangements made

"....no difference whatsoever to school relationships".

This sentiment was echoed at all stages and one comment from the 1960's group suggested that there was

".....no awareness at all of bursaries or foundations or fee paying people - it was never discussed although no secrecy was involved".

Rather than causing divisions within the school, for some former pupils the tradition of bursaries, foundations and scholarships created a perceived difference between Gordon's and Aberdeen Grammar School. Some reference will be made later to the intense rivalry between these two historic educational institutions. For Ian Hustwick (1932-41) the Grammar was for the sons of

".....middle class professional people, whereas Gordon's had more bursaries and foundations and attracted more lower middle class pupils".

"Buff" Hardie (1943-49) gives a similar view when he says,

"Gordon's got a lot more people like myself. I came from Hilton - one of the Corporation primary schools. I was never actually quite sure to what extent the Grammar School was fee paying but I think more people there paid fees of one kind or another. So it tended to be a bit more middle class and I suppose we thought, 'toffee-nosed' !"

The coming of comprehensivisation in the 1960's has, in the opinion of many contributors, reduced the elite status of the Grammar School. Thus Gordon's is now seen to be the more middle class (toffee-nosed!!) institution.

As we will see, it was far from the case that all pupils receiving financial assistance had a happy time at Gordon's, but the consensus seems to be that the scholarship tradition at Gordon's not only benefited many of the sons of the less well off families but also gave the College a real social mix. Few would go so far as to say that the Gordon's community today reflects the social diversity of several decades ago. Nevertheless, as a result of an appeal in the 1970's and the latest appeal launched in 1996, the College Governors have been able to "top up" the funds available for scholarships by approximately one million pounds and thus continue the tradition regarded so highly by former pupils.

Chapter 2

Buildings and Classrooms

Having passed through the main entrance to the College the abiding memory of many of those nervous pupils entering the school for the first time was not so much the architectural beauty of the Auld Hoose but, in the words of one, *" Cannons and Huts "*. The cannons were two Russian artillery pieces captured during the Crimean War which stood on either side of the entrance to the Auld Hoose. They provided much interest and amusement for pupils right up to the time of their removal in the early part of the Second World War, when it was felt that the metal should contribute to this greater conflict. According to one pupil of the 1940's the cannons were covered in grease because, *"You used to sit on them to eat your pie"*. The huts were more commonly referred to as the *"Tin Palaces"* which were put up during the First World War and were features of school life throughout the 1920's. According to John Cruickshank (1926-1932) these huts were

> *".....dark, not too many windows...Greasy Bob taught there".*

The *"Tin Palaces"* were taken away during the building of the MacRobert Hall and more use was made of Crooked Lane accommodation.

"The School Surrenders its Guns !"

In the 1930's the basement of Crooked Lane was used for practical workshops such as Woodwork, with History and English classrooms above. Classics occupied the upper rooms of the East Wing. According to John Reid (1930-36), who gave much information on classroom accommodation, the Auld Hoose housed Music in room 28 along with French (room 25) and Maths (room 24). Modern Languages were also taught in rooms 9 and 10 with rooms 7 and 8 used for Art. In rooms numbered 21, 22 and 23 English and Commerce were taught. The top floor of the West Wing provided accommodation for Primary 5, 6 and 7 classes, although earlier, according to Alexander Gray (1912-17) who attended the College from the age of ten,

> *"....the lowest two classes were Primary A and Primary B which were both located on the top (4th floor) of the Auld Hoose."*

In room 1 French was taught; room 2 was English; room 3 was History; room 4 was Geography and in room 6 Maths was taught. The MacRobert Hall was opened in 1931 and morning assemblies there became another memorable, if not always enjoyable, feature of daily life at the College. The Hall also came to house the school library (formerly a small collection of books at the back of a classroom in the West Wing) until the opening of the present library in 1968.

The First College Library - Opened Founder's Day 1938

What today is the General Office was, in the 1930's and 1940's, the Staff Room and the Head's Study was what is now the Cash Office. It is interesting to note that the School Office adjacent to the Head's Study was, up to the 1960's, occupied by only one full time secretary (many remember Miss Cowl) and an assistant who, according to several former pupils, ran the school ! Also on the ground floor, occupying what is now a Guidance room and the Development Office, was the Ladies Staff Room where, rumour has it, the only two ladies on the senior school staff in the 1950's did not speak to each other ! From the 1940's the old room 4 in the West Wing (where the College "library" had been located) became the Main Staff Room. Ladies were not admitted until the 1970's ! The Prefects' Room was what was, until recently, the Interview Room but is now occupied by the Administration System Manager.

The Second World War did, as we will see later, affect the daily life of the College. However one of the first indications, for the pupils, of forthcoming dangers was the digging up of the grass at the front of the school and the building of the air raid shelters. For the pupils of the 1940's the ability of the shelters to offer real protection was questionable to say the least. According to Alan Kennedy (1938-41) their construction was

> *".....a token contribution towards providing sheltered accommodation for the total number of pupils",*

whilst Arthur McCombie (1940-46) asks,

> *"Was it not just timber with turf over the top. I mean it wasn't even metal or anything !".*

Indeed the structural inadequacies of the shelters seemed to be confirmed at one morning assembly by the then Headmaster, David Collier, who, according to *"Buff"* Hardie (1943-49), said,

> *" I must ask you to be more careful and less noisy going down the stairs to the shelter, they're not constructed to withstand that kind of treatment" !!*

Unlike many other buildings in Aberdeen, the school was largely unaffected by wartime bombing. A bomb did explode very close to the front of the Auld Hoose but, apart from some broken windows, the main block was untouched. Indeed Arthur McCombie goes on to record that,

" The amazing thing about the bomb was how the stuff was thrown right over the building. Heckie Donaldson's room had a glass roof and it was covered with debris, and the front and back playground was covered with debris, and, apart from this bloody great hole, there was nothing ! I think it had been the soft ground and of course the tarmac that had kind of sealed it in a bit...".

The Building of the Air-raid Shelters 1939
Photograph courtesy of Aberdeen Journals

Recollections regarding the buildings often return to the well worn steps of the Auld Hoose where generations of Gordon's pupils have trudged up and, probably much more light-heartedly, have skipped down. Several mentions have been made of the upper classrooms of Crooked lane with their

"knotted floorboards in a convex shape".

The 1960's group remember the building of the Science Block but were generally unimpressed by its square, steel and concrete structure - *"....just a box"*. The durability of the Science Block has been questioned by later pupils who remember cracks appearing in the walls. Indeed the construction of the Blackfriars Building in the early 1990's was, according to one source,

"....mainly to prop up the Science Block !".

"The Well Worn Steps of the Auld Hoose 1968"
Photograph courtesy of Aberdeen Journals

The Blackfriars Building which was opened for use in 1993 greatly increased facilities by providing a new Dining Room (formerly housed on the ground floor of the Junior School and prior to that under a building adjacent to the MacRobert Hall), Staff Room, Conference Room, Sixth Year Area and numerous classrooms. However the 1990's group, whilst acknowledging the importance of these additions, were somewhat cynical of the attempts to make it blend in with the older parts of the school,

".....it failed miserably because for the first three years of its existence there were these enormous yellow pipes up the side of the building !".

Of course whatever the architectural merits of the Blackfriars Building, a four storey block has one over-riding disadvantage which was succinctly explained by one member of the 1990's group -

" You're knackered by the time you get to the top of it"!

The Dining Room 1962 - *Photograph courtesy of Scottish Field*

Chapter 3

The School Day

The means by which pupils travelled to and from school has clearly changed over time. In the early decades of this century those boys who lived near to the school could walk, but for those who lived further away the choice was trams or bicycles. The much greater use of bikes in the early part of the century is reflected in the comments of one 1920's pupil who estimates that the cycle sheds at the back of the Art Gallery contained well over 200 bikes, none of which were locked - *" Nobody stole bicycles in those days".* Use of the Aberdeen trams continued through the 1950's although buses were increasingly used by College pupils. In 1955 one country pupil arrived on a Fordson tractor with plough attached, and, according to a contemporary, drove it round the perimeter of the grass at the front of the school while a nervous janitor shouted, *" Dinna drap the ploo !"* Such forms of transport were exceptional but even motor cars were still few and far between in the 1950's and 1960's. Evidence for this is the fact that several former pupils remember Jimmy Geals, the Latin master, coming to school in a pre-war Humber, registration number AV 8187. Duncan Munro (1960-69) remembers a Morris 1100, registration number MRS 2, which used to draw up at the school, *"......but that was about it".* One opinion of the 1960's group was that boys who were dropped off in the morning by car *"......were considered effeminate"!* By the 1970's and 1980's cycling to and from school was becoming less common and today the bike shed is used by relatively few pupils. Travel by bus and car is now most common and the latter has clearly lost the stigma of the 1960's !

In the early part of the century daily registration, according to Alexander Gray (1912-17), involved the Headmaster visiting

> *"...each class once every day and he entered the number of boys into a huge ledger which he carried with him....He became a familiar figure to the boys."*

From the 1930's the school day started with assembly in the MacRobert Hall. For many pupils this offered the only contact with the Headmaster who by this time came across as a very distant authority figure. Pupils in the 1930's and 1940's, as today, sat in classes, sang a hymn and listened to a reading from one of the prefects. At the end of the assembly form captains would be expected to check attendance with the instruction - *"call the roll !"*. Much respected English teacher A.S. *"Sandy"* Fraser, and later swimming instructor Andrew *"Andy"* Robb, came to be responsible for the well ordered entry and exit from the Hall. According to a respondent of the 1950's

"....if you missed assembly you had to queue downstairs and get one of the belt from Mr. Collier".

Those of a different religious persuasion were allowed to miss assembly. It is reported that in the 1950's one Davie Cruickshank

".....decided to become a catholic - they never found out even though his brother attended assembly !"

Few pupils appear to have enjoyed assemblies but the occasional naive announcement would enliven proceedings such as Dr. Forrest's memorable pronouncement as Deputy Head in the 1960's that,

" Senior pupils are not allowed to interfere with Junior pupils' balls in the back playground".

An increasing school roll meant that by the 1980's the MacRobert Hall could not accommodate the whole senior school, and so pupils, as today, attended morning assembly only up to three days per week. The general lack of interest in assemblies was also felt in the Junior school where Sarah Wyatt, one of the first two Primary 1 girls to join the College in 1989, records that class assembly in P1 was

"....quite boring and we usually found something else to amuse ourselves - rolling our socks down for instance".

Such is the ingenuity and adaptability of the Gordon's pupil !

As well as being allocated to one of the four school Houses - Sillerton, Straloch, Blackfriars or Collyhill, pupils from S1 were put into ability classes ranging from A to E. This system of streaming continued largely unchanged up to the 1980's. After one month in the school "re-grading" exams. took place and thereafter "divisional" examinations determined a pupil's stream for the next year. From the 1930's through to the 1980's former pupils have commented on the division created between those intelligent enough to do Latin and those who were not allowed to do it. For much of this time the D and E classes did technical subjects such as Woodwork and Metalwork

Assembly in the MacRobert Hall 1962
Photograph courtesy of Scottish Field

instead of Latin. Much bitterness and dissatisfaction has been expressed at the academic elitism shown by the staff. For those boys in the D and E classes there was, according to one pupil of the 1930's,

".....the feeling that the staff were not bothered".

The 1940's group expressed surprise and dismay at a system which rejected someone of the talent of Jack Webster who was asked to leave Gordon's at the age of fourteen to then go on to become one of Scotland's foremost journalists - and be invited back as Founder's Day Speaker in 1997 ! Another common source of criticism to come through was the lack of counselling - either academic or pastoral - available to pupils, and this theme runs through the the responses from the 1920's to the 1960's. Similarly feedback to parents was, compared to the 1990's, very limited. Such contact was limited to Report Cards which, in the 1950's for example, were handed out by the Headmaster Mr. Collier, who, like his predecessor Mr Graham Andrew, would come into class and give them to the boys individually along with some brief comment. According to some this was *".....the only time we spoke to him!"* Even in the 1960's respondents could not recall regular parents meetings. In the 1980's streaming ended and a system of broad banding was introduced for S1 and S2 and which has now been superseded by mixed ability groups. A structured guidance system and the concept of staff-parent "partnership" has gone some way towards overcoming some of the problems experienced in preceding decades.

It is probably as true today as in the past that, for many pupils, the bright spots in the day are the breaks for morning interval and lunch. One of the great attractions of break in the early days was the time it afforded the boys to buy buns and, in particular, the fondly remembered pie. It is the opinion of John Cruickshank (1926-32) that Mitchell and Muil's pies, sold in school at one penny each,

"......were the best pies I ever tasted...".

The bun queue under the pillars at the side of the Auld Hoose was a very popular and sometimes dangerous place in the 1940's as indicated by J. Sutherland's illustration in the 1945 issue of the Gordonian. It is indicative of the priorities of the Gordon's pupil that so much has been said about pies. Indeed a literary contribution to the 1946 Gordonian reinforces their hallowed place in the memories of so many Gordonians -

TO A PIE

Wee, squishy, drippen' bit o' pasty,

O fit's in thee that is sae tasty

That I maun gobble thee sae hasty

Wi' watterin' mou'?

I wad be laith tae hae tae waste thee

When no sae fu'!

(Gobble, gobble, gobble !)

S. Johnston IIIb

The Bun Queue - some things never change!

The bun queue tradition has continued to the present day even although the venue may have changed over time along with the suppliers of pies, doughnuts, sticky buns, etc. However, in addition to consuming vast quantities of delightfully unhealthy food, break time has always been a time for boys in the senior school to play football in the back playground - some displaying a passion never witnessed in the classroom ! Unfortunately participation in a less healthy pastime was also a fact of life at Gordon's. The outside toilets in the corner of the playground, where the Blackfriars building now stands, was the *"smokers retreat"*. Other meeting places have been mentioned such as the bike sheds, etc., although many pupils recall the door of the Main Staff Room opening to reveal a *".....pall of smoke"*. It is interesting to note that, in line with national trends, the number of boys smoking has declined over the past ten to fifteen years years - and the Staff Room is now a smoke - free zone !

Football in the Back Playground (before the Blackfriars Building)

In the early part of the century most boys went home for lunch. Country pupils and others who lived further out brought packed lunches or bought food in town. Whilst in town the pupils of the 20's and 30's would have come across one of the great characters of the Aberdeen streets - *"Fool Friday"*. Fool (or dirty) Friday was an Italian who sold ice cream in summer and roast chestnuts in winter from a barrow on Schoolhill. Most pupils do indeed remember him as being filthy and William Sinclair (1924-27) talks of his skin being *"...engraved like a crocodile's."* It wasn't until 1944 that the College started providing lunches at 4d per meal. The quality of the meals in those early days is difficult to judge. According to Ian Hunter (1945-48) they were

> *"......very good. A pal of mine was organising it and I used to get seconds all the time".*

However Douglas Davidson (1944-50) says,

> *"I went once and that was it. I took the bike home after that!"*

As today, some pupils took the opportunity not only to eat out of school, but also to look round the shops. For one of the trendier 1950's group it was a chance to keep up with the latest musical developments,

> *" We used to go down to Isaac Benzie's and listen to the latest Elvis Presley record in the booths there".*

"Fool Friday"
Photograph courtesy of Aberdeen Journals

For a handful of pupils the daily routine at school was made difficult by some bullying by other pupils. This tended to be a fact of life in almost all schools in years past and although the vast majority of interviewees had no knowledge or experience of it, isolated incidents at Schoolhill have been described. One of the 1970's pupils remembers one boy who

> *"....used to wear a Crombie coat and Doc. Marten's and that was the sign of a hard man, shaved head, and he was the school bully, we were all a bit scared of him".*

The pupils of the 1980's and 1990's felt generally that what bullying there was occurred in S1 and S2 but died out *"....as we grew older we all matured".*

Another much more recognisable element of day to day life at Gordon's was, and still is, the uniform. Surprisingly perhaps, uniformity of dress, as required today, was not so evident before the 1950's and 1960's. Although navy blazers were worn in the 1920's by most pupils in S1 and S2 there was a fair degree of latitude for older pupils as the selection of Prefects photographs indicates. In the 1940's most S5 and S6 pupils wore sports jackets and flannels. Rationing was a main factor in having less rigid rules at this time. Shorts were often worn by senior pupils up to S3 and even beyond. Kilts were sometimes preferred by pupils like Sandy Lunan (1953-58),

> *" I didn't have a long pair of trousers until six months after I'd left school. I wore the kilt all the time".*

The option of sports jackets for S6 pupils was still there in the 1950's although by that time blazers for senior pupils were more common and shorts and caps were part of the uniform for boys in S1 and S2. It is interesting to note that the 1960's and 1970's witnessed the greatest difficulties in terms of regulating the appearance of pupils. "Beatlemania" had popularised longer hair for boys and the then Headmaster, Mr John *"Jack"* Marshall, and his staff had to battle hard to keep hair to acceptable length. By the 1970's flared trousers and platform shoes were also fashion items which added to the conflict ! The 1980's and 1990's boys' fashion preference for shorter hair and "regular" fitting trousers have made the life of the teachers much easier. The regulation kilt for the girls has also made variation of appearance less likely.

The College Prefects

1939-40

1948-49

1955-56

1973-74

1995-96

1997-98

Janitors William Murray and Charles Craig

Daily routine in school cannot be fully considered without reference to the janitors. The pupils of the 20's and early 30's remember Charles Murray,

> *"...a handsome figure..who always put his left finger in his ear when he blew the whistle for assembly."*

It was Mr. Murray's daughter who presented the painting of her father, whistle in hand, to the school. His likeness can still be seen hanging on the wall on the ground floor of the Auld Hoose, adjacent to the Medical Room. Rather less striking and more a figure of fun for the boys was Charlie Craig who succeeded Mr. Murray in 1936. *"Buff"* Hardie (1943-49) recalls Charlie being called to attend to a broken window in one of the classrooms. Having examined the damage he confirmed, much to the amusement of the boys,

> *"Aye, it's broken - on both sides !"*

Finally, some mention should be made of one or two significant breaks in the daily routine, which a number of former pupils have remarked upon. When World War 2 broke out the pupils at the College were required to attend for half days only - either mornings or afternoons. This arrangement only lasted for a short time until air raid shelters were deemed sufficient to house all the pupils. Several of the 1940's group remember filling sandbags down at the harbour although there were other significant contributions made as illustrated. Boys were also involved in fire watching duties with staff on the roof of the Auld Hoose. Edgar Allan (1930-42) says,

The Boys Help With the Harvest 1939
Recorded in the Bon-Accord

"I used to fire watch in the school.....We had a bucket and stirrup pump. What we would have done if anything happened goodness knows !"

Another interruption to the normal daily routine occurred with the typhoid outbreak of 1964. Periods were reduced to 20 minutes and pupils got home in the afternoon unless they were involved in games at Seafield. This free time was referred to as the *"typhoid holidays"* and one of the 1960's group remembers that,

"Vast numbers of us, children generally, went down to the beach during the typhoid holidays, while the rest of the country was told we were sitting inside our houses waiting for the curse to come along and people shouting 'bring out your dead'."

Class Photos

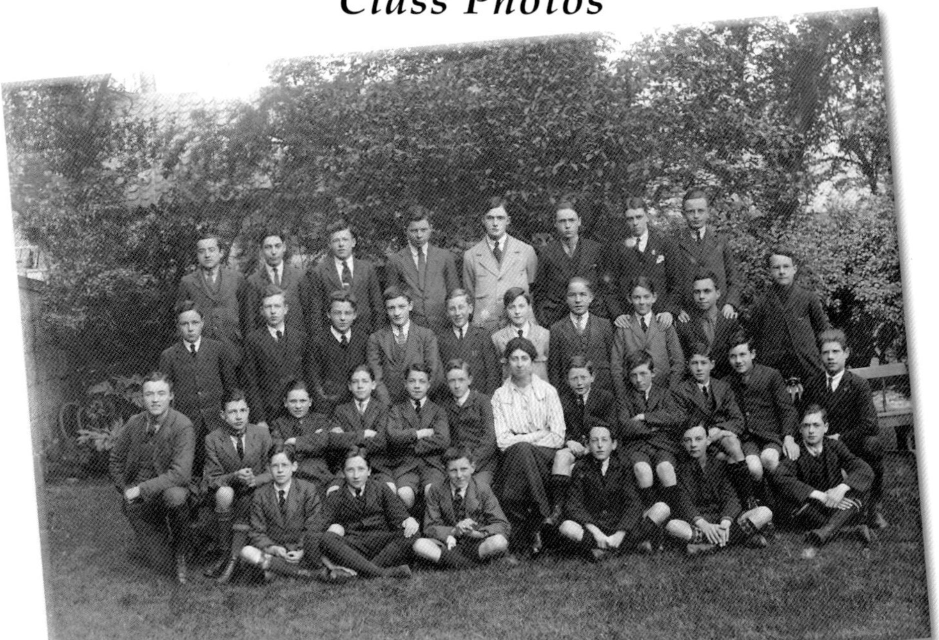

3A 1918-19

1C 1929-30

5B/C 1937-38

3E 1966-7

5M 1994-5

Chapter 4

Teachers

Of all the varied memories and recollections, the greatest number by far relate to the teachers. As indicated earlier, these memories display fondness, admiration, respect, gratitude, etc., but also, in some cases, unhappiness, fear and even loathing. Like other educational institutions in the earlier decades of this century, Gordon's imposed strict discipline on its pupils and this, until the 1980's, included physical punishment mainly in the form of the "belt". However, apart from memories of belting and other forms of punishment, the thing that stands out most is the use of nicknames. Unlike today, almost all teachers acquired a nickname.

William Sinclair (1924-27) recalls that discipline was *"pretty severe, but very fair"*, with the use of the belt very common and he remembers being beaten by George *"Fiery"* Forbes. Mr. Forbes and some of the other male staff who were at Gordon's before the First World War can be seen in the photograph of the 1913 staff football team. The full staff photograph of 1923 includes more of those depicted in less formal terms in this account. One teacher appearing on both of these photographs is Alexander Booth - *"Boothie"*. Mr. Booth taught Geography at the school for over forty years. More will be said later of his contribution to extra-curricular activities, but the 1920's pupils remember him, when belting pupils, putting a duster on the wrist to stop the blow causing blue blisters ! The 1930's pupils recall Boothie's classroom windows being blacked out as he used a "magic lantern" for most of his teaching. John Mackintosh - *"Johnny Mack"*- the Head of History who also spent most of his teaching career at the school is described by many as an *"exceptional teacher"*. Mr. Mackintosh wrote two textbooks on British and European History which became prescribed reading for Gordon's pupils.

As in all areas of life, the First World War cast a long shadow over the school. Alexander Gray (1912-17) recalls the early days of the war,

> *"Several of our teachers had Officers Commissions from their days at university and were called up to active duty as Reservists. The Gordon Highlanders used the playground as a drill field and the boys used to stand during the intervals and watch our own teachers marching up and down..."*

The Staff Football Team 1913

Those teachers who survived the war - in common with most "old" soldiers of that terrible conflict - never talked to the boys about their experiences. One young Maths teacher, William *"Knockers"* Murray, suffered the effects of shell shock for the remainder of his life although his pupils responded to this in a less than sympathetic way ! His colleague in the Maths Department and fellow war veteran, Robert Stewart - *"Greasy Bob"*- would *"look after"* Knockers if there was too much noise in the adjacent classroom. *"Greasy Bob"* was the unofficial careers master and was renowned for his loud voice and his (inaccurate) chalk throwing ! However one former pupil, regretting the treatment of Mr. Murray penned this remorseful poem -

Batty

"Batty", they called him. Fussing his charge
of boys, he sat before them at each school assembly,
small, spidery and bald - his patent skull
an egg-shell, paper-thin, clinically fragile.

They said he suffered badly in the war.

Boys are cruel. The sniping and bombardment
of the class were no less deadly:
the enemy, entrenched at loaded desks,
ambushed the blackboard, attacked down enfiladed corridors.

Til skull cracked wide, spilt its yolk of terror.

How many Batty boys, themselves grown
desperate and gray, trapped in life's decay,
rising every morning fraught and lone-
assembling to confront the ambuscade-
now remember him and groan ?

Ken Morrice (1936-41)

Another effect of the call to arms of men during the Great War was the need for female "labour". Gordon's College was no exception. During the war Miss Ellenor Herbert- *"Skinny Liz"*- arrived to teach English and Drama, and Miss Catherine Mackenzie - *"Squeezy"*- taught French. The latter's nickname derived somehow from *"excusez moi"* - perhaps telling us something of the standard of spoken French among the pupils ! Miss Mackenzie's teaching method, according to one source, involved a

> *"...vocabulary book in one hand and a belt in the other..."*.

A little later Miss Jane Fraser - *"Bunty"*- joined the staff to teach Modern Languages and Miss Jean Smith - *"Moosie"*- arrived to teach Latin - the latter soon gaining the reputation as *" a belter"*.

A great character on the staff, and featured in the title of this book, was William Grant Thomson - *"Long Tom"*. Mr. Thomson was another veteran of the war who, at about 6'6" tall, towered over his colleagues as well as his pupils. He was not averse to using the belt - indeed he is reputed to have had a *"selection"* from which pupils could choose ! He is remembered as having the *"...biggest bicycle in Aberdeen.."* which had an unusual double cross-bar. Long Tom was considered to be a gentleman with almost naive good manners which was inevitably exploited by the boys. According to one pupil of the 1940's group,

> *"....he used to cycle through the gateway of the school and the joke was that he would always respond to little boys who saluted, and of course he did the same and nearly fell off his bike, and this was the thing they enjoyed doing"*.

Edgar Allan (1930-42) adds,

> *"...one day some of the boys were standing with some girls from the Central School and so, not only had he to return the salutes, he also had to lift his hat to the ladies and fell off his bike completely !"*

Another Thomson remembered by the pupils of the 1920's and 1930's was James *"Devil"* Thomson who, as Ronald McLeod (1927-35) recalls, belted a whole class of 28 boys for not getting the right solution to a problem - only to find that he had set the wrong piece of work ! Science teacher James Gordon, known as *"Pudner"*, by contrast, never used the belt but was one of the *".. most feared men in the school"*, according to the 1940's group, largely because of his *"withering sarcasm"*. George *"Hoot"* Gibson (named after a

A Gordonian's Nightmare

James Thomson (Maths.) | George Morrison (Headmaster) | Emil Lentz (French)

William Copland (Latin) | M. A. Young (Typist) | M. W. Murray (French) | Edward Hay (French)

W. Murray (Janitor)

The Unhappy Pupil | Theo. Fairley (Sports)

The Artist is Herbert W. Milne (Div. VI.)

cowboy film star), who succeeded William *"Fat Bill"* Copland as Head of Classics, is remembered as a very strict teacher who taught effectively through a mixture of fear, respect and some affection. Another interesting character featured in both the *"Gordonian's Nightmare"* from 1921 and the 1923 staff photograph, is Emil Lentz. Having won the Medaille Militaire and the Croix de Guerre in the First World War, *"Lentils"* was appointed as assistante in the Modern Languages Department. After the fall of France in the Second World War he became local consul for the Committee of Liberation and, after the war, left the College to become French Consul-adjoint in Southampton.

English teacher John *"Frosty"* Foster was a very flamboyant character, both in terms of his clothes - coloured shirts and bow ties - and in his teaching method. If, for example, *"Frosty"* was teaching King Lear he wouldn't bother with notes, he would act the parts. His thespian accomplishments were also displayed in the productions of the *"Auld Hoose"* - "Frosty" of course played the part of Robert Gordon ! A teacher, again by contrast, remembered with considerably less affection was Maths teacher and later the Head of Mathemetics, *"Davy"* Donald. Situated in room 6 overlooking the back quadrangle, Mr. Donald was renowned for confiscating footballs, belting pupils with an enjoyment bordering on sadism and is described by several former pupils as simply *"terrifying"*. Head of Music from the late 1920's to the 1940's, Joseph *"Holy Joe"* Kimberly Smith, is remembered by most for producing fine concerts in the Music Hall and by some for his Austin 7 motor car. Mr.M.W. Murray is recalled for his close cropped hair - hence the nickname *"Convict"*. Maths teacher Mr. Charles Lee is remembered by some for hiding his wooden blackboard duster up the sleeve of his gown and throwing it at unsuspecting pupils. Jimmy Geals in the Classics Department had a similar preference for this (mis)use of the blackboard duster - as well as a reputation as *"a belter"*. It was rumoured in the 1960's that he had even broken a boy's wrist !

As indicated already, the pupils of the earlier part of the century found the Headmasters rather distant figures. However Mr. Graham Andrew is acknowledged by many puils of the 1930's and 40's as a great innovator. Robert Bruce (1934-40) records that it was during his tenure of office that the College got

"....the swimming pool, Founder's Day, the prefect system, class captains, interscholastic sports and improved rugby fixtures".

It is interesting to note that the Otaki Scholarship also dates from this time. Mention has already been made of Dr. Forrest who, as Head of English, had a keen interest in debating and was highly regarded by his pupils as was his predecessor Walter Humphries. Art teacher Robert *"Baldy"* Murray is remembered as a *"...brilliant enthusiast.."* Mr. Murray managed to maintain his enthusiasm despite the efforts of some of the 1930's pupils who attempted to disrupt his lessons. Ronald McLeod (1929-35) remembers his classmates collecting a few pennies to bribe an Italian street seller to play his organ in Crooked Lane where it could be heard through *"Baldy's"* almost permanently open windows,

"...but I think he realised something was up because it happened so often, we gave up in the end!"

George Barton, Geography teacher, Head of the Junior School is also remembered with fond respect by his former pupils. Mr. Barton's duties as the first Boarding House Master are referred to later. The reputation of swimming instructor Andy Robb is little short of legendary and more will also be said of him later.

One interesting feature of the immediate post-Second World War period for many pupils was the recollections of teachers who had served in the forces. Unlike the old soldiers of the First World War who, as indicated above, never spoke about their experiences, the veterans of this later conflict were more than happy to tell of theirs. Indeed, according to one of the 1950's group,

"...you could always get them talking and avoid doing Latin, etc...."

One member of staff who had been a Marine Commando *"...taught us how to kill a guy.."* Even in the 1970's we are told that,

"Mr. Sutherland would tell us tales of being a wireless operator in a World War II bomber".

For the pupils of the 1960's and 1970's few staff are mentioned without the invariable nicknames such as Charles *"Beaky"* Morton, Miss *"Cherrylips"* McLean, John *"Tinky"* Reid, John *"Goofy"* Gordon, *"Fritz"* Ballard, Ian *"Spinner"* McKenzie, etc. Although still restricted to the Ladies Staff Room or *"Wifies Howff"*, the number of female teachers was increasing at this time. For example the attractions of the Music Department were not entirely restricted to the commitment and enthusiasm of Douglas Tees, but also we are told, the *"attributes"* of Miss Cecilia Cavaye and later Miss Rhonda Shand. Nevertheless discipline was considered to be strict and the belt was still widely used in the 1970's. Ian *"Spike"* Calder is remembered as

"a great badminton player and the best belter in the school!"

One primary pupil of the late 1970's describes the discipline in school as *"draconian"* and recalls a fellow pupil having his mouth washed out with soap and water for swearing. The Headmaster Jack Marshall is remembered and greatly respected as a strict disciplinarian. This was often translated and recorded for posterity on desks and walls (allegedly including one in Switzerland !) as, *"JAXARAJ"*. Some staff are remembered for their oft repeated phrases. One of the 1970's group reminds us of Classics teacher Mr. Urwin Woodman's end of lesson instructions,

"Well, goodbye men. Pack away your goods and chattels and be on your merry way !"

By the 1980's and 90's, in spite of reference to the likes of *"Zoot"* McColgan, *"Blinky"* Dewar, etc., it would appear that nicknames were less commonly used. Why this should be the case remains a mystery. Although this ties in with the ending of the use of the belt in 1985, the connection between the two is questionable. The standard of teaching was in the view of Gordon Fergus (1981-87) *"..spot on.."* although

"...discipline was strict and the staff still called you by your surname".

The latter appears to have ended when the girls arrived in 1989, and the tradition of saluting staff was also becoming a thing of the past. Old habits die hard however and Graham Sangster (1964-72) tells of his embarrassment when attending his first assembly as a newly appointed teacher in the late 1970's. When the Headmaster dismissed the boys in the customary way, Graham, sitting at the back with other members of staff, stood bolt upright and saluted !

Some respondents would argue that there have been fewer characters and eccentrics on the staff in the last couple of decades of the millennium. However from the 1990's group stories are legion regarding Ian *"The Rev."* Prior,

"For our first year exam. he made us write out the Lord's Prayer and mark it ourselves. We all got full marks !"

Walter *"Wally"* Craig is often quoted with his great passion for Aberdeen Football Club. John *"J.J."* Jermieson is another great Gordon's character, fondly remembered by the pupils, even although he ruled with *"a rod of iron"* from room 6. Melanie Marshall (1992-97) also recalls

"...this ageing hippy called Dr. Gotts. He was absolutely great, he was so cool...He would let us listen to Bob Dylan and the Beatles and analyse the lyrics like they were poetry !"

Finally, of the headmasters of the last two decades, less has been said because they tend to figure less in the day to day lives of ordinary pupils. Recalling Mr. George Allan, Sarah Wyatt - one of the first girls in P1 - says he was,

"....a big scary person who we never saw, only heard about. We thought he was the owner of the school and could do whatever he wanted..."

but she goes on to add that, having met him, he was *"...very nice"*. The pupils of the 1990's recognise and acknowledge the efforts of Mr. Brian Lockhart to be as *"..visible and approachable.."* as possible although one said,

"He sat down at the dinner table and spoke to us but we didn't know what to do !"

The College Staff

1923

1936

1959

1968

1989

Chapter 5

Sports and extra - curricular activities

In the early part of the century sporting standards at Gordon's were not of the highest order. However from the 1930's - and based to a large extent on the work of Mr. J.A. Kerr Hunter as Head of Physical Education - the reputation of the College was greatly enhanced. Sport became a nationally recognised strength and a significant number of comments by former pupils refer to this area of school life. These comments reflect the achievements of the school in the main sporting activities such as rugby, hockey, swimming, athletics, etc. They also bear testimony to the commitment and hard work of staff as well as the increasingly impressive sporting facilities available to the pupils. However at the beginning of the century facilities at the Schoolhill site were very limited and became even more so with the outbreak of World War 1. Alexander Gray (1912-17) remembers that between 1914 and 1918,

> *"...a lot of our school buildings and playgrounds were taken over by the soldiers for training. Just prior to our summer holidays we had our Sports Day and since we had no playing field to do our running, the playing fields of Kings College in Old Aberdeen were made available to us."*

Football Team late 1920's

Gordon's produced successful football teams up to the 1950's but football ceased to be an "official" sporting activity in the second half of the century although the emphasis on rugby as the main winter sport has not appealed to all. However the insistence that the boys play the game from P6 through to the early years of senior school - as is still the case today - has contributed to the ongoing reputation of Gordon's College as one of Scotland's foremost rugby schools.This reputation has been built on the enthusiasm of members of staff like Sandy Fraser who, according to a number of respondents, had *"a massive influence"* on rugby in the 1940's. The playing fields at Seafield have - until the move to Countesswells in 1991 (officially opened in 1992) - witnessed many memorable rugby moments. However according to the pupils of the 20's and 30's the pitches at Seafield were often in poor condition.As Bill Brown (1926-32) recalls,

> *"....when we went up to Seafield to play rugby, the first thing we had to do was to line up shoulder to shoulder and walk round the pitch with little containers picking up stones and pieces of glass and what have you, and that was done every week."*

1st XV 1937-8

For boys keen on rugby, progression - as today - through the *"Minors"*, *"Juniors"* and *"Colts"* might mean an opportunity to play for the First XV. Indeed many went on to play first class rugby with Gordonians and some - like Bert Bruce (1934 - 40) - to play for Scotland. Two of the highlights of the sporting calendar up to the 1960's were the home and away fixtures against arch-rivals the Grammar School. *"Buff"* Hardie recalls that,

> *"Almost the whole of both schools turned out. It was an extra-ordinary crowd for those matches. Great occasions!"*

In S4 the boys have always been allowed to make a choice between rugby and hockey although this has never satisfied all sporting preferences. Colin Johnston (1961-67) tells the story of the Head of P.E. George *"Jock"* Hastie instructing the boys at Seafield to separate into two groups - those opting for hockey and those opting for rugby. Each group was sent off, leaving one boy still waiting. When asked what he was going to do he replied,

> *" I'm going to be a professional footballer."*

The boy, Martin Buchan, was quickly and unsympathetically dispatched but went on, not only to achieve his ambition, but to captain Aberdeen, Manchester United and win 34 caps for Scotland ! A further illustration of the less than whole hearted commitment to playing with the oval ball is provided by Stephen Witte (1986 - 98) when he says,

> *"I wish rugby had never been invented. It's overplayed - it's ridiculous. On snow covered pitches they make you go out in shorts and fall down and get stamped on. It's stupid!"*

Swimming is another sport for which Gordon's has become nationally recognised. Prior to the opening of the College swimming pool in 1937 some coaching had been available and the Annual Gala was held at the Beach Baths. However things rapidly developed with the coming of Andy Robb as superintendent of the new pool in 1938 and his later appointment as Swimming Instructor. Not only were innumerable trophies won but pupils went on to represent Scotland, Britain and - in the case of Athole Still and Iain Black (world record holder and silver medal winner in 1960) - to compete in the Olympic Games. Former pupils have pointed out that in addition to his achievements in coaching swimming and various organisational duties in school, he gave up his summer holidays to organise and run various camps - initially taking over Finzean camp from Mr. Booth. As one perspicacious former pupil of the 1940's says,

> *" The thing about Andy Robb was, apart from his expertise as a swimming coach, he was a wonderful schoolmaster. He participated in all the events, and he organised everything. I always suspected that there must have been a bit of rivalry or worse between him and the P.E. staff!"*

The comments of several Gordonians who attended the school in the 40's, 50's and 60's suggest that, for them, the swimming pool and Andy Robb's reputation as a coach were the key reasons for choosing to come to Gordon's.

Andy Robb's Life-Saving Class 1947

Another great encouragement to participate in extra-curricular sport at the college arose with the opening up of the facilities at Seafield on Tuesday, Wednesday and Thursday evenings during the summer term where *"vast numbers of masters"* helped with cricket, athletics, etc. The pupils of the 1940's recall the various athletics tournaments involving the University, Grammar and Gordon's which also attracted large crowds. Howard Smith (1949-60)

Athletics 1948

remembers the inter-class cricket matches held on these evenings,

> *".....organised by the classes themselves and no class had a problem getting its eleven out."*

Tennis, badminton, basketball and other sports have been mentioned by the pupils as has hockey which also claims a strong part of Gordon's sporting tradition - both for boys and, since 1989, for girls. Of course, just as some of the boys have been less than fascinated with rugby, so some of the girls reacted against hockey, especially, in the words of one 1990's pupil, when you had to wear

> *".....horrible hockey skirts that made your bum look enormous."*

In addition to team and individual sports where excellence has always been recognised with *"colours"* awards, a vast range of other extra-curricular activities has always been offered by the College. John Cruickshank (1926-32) recalls Mr. Booth, the Geography teacher, organising various day trips to such places as Stonehaven, Bennachie, etc.,

> *"...and I can remember five charabancs at the front gates there, and they were the real old charabancs, a door for each row of seats, like a toast rack, and we went to Lochnagar.....some of them broke down before we got as*

1st XI Hockey 1979

1st XI Girls Hockey 1996

far as Loch Muick....over a hundred boys must have gone. It was mostly first years."

Also in the late 20's *"Boothie"* went on to organise the annual school camp at Finzean, on the south bank of the Feugh opposite the Bucket Mill. He would spend almost the whole summer holiday supervising the boys with the help of other members of staff such as Mr. Kerr Hunter and Mr. Mackintosh, and the boys could attend for as long as they wished. The hut at Finzean which was presented by the Gordonian Association in the late 30's afforded the boys some more permanent storage and accommodation in bad weather. In addition to the normal tasks allocated to the boys, Eric Auld (1943-48) recalls another,

> *"I used to go to Finzean for school camp. Boothie was resident there and some people were delegated to take him back from the Feughside Inn !"*

As indicated above Andy Robb went on to organise and supervise the camp after Boothie's retiral.

The 1930's also saw what some recall as being the first trips abroad for the pupils. John Croll (1926 - 1936) remembers a cruise to Scandinavia,

> *"...I think it cost us £14 for the fortnight...it was in 1936 when things were getting a bit difficult and we went through the Keil Canal and we noticed the preparations of a certain country even in 1936."*

A trip the next year actually included travel in Germany and Austria. Interestingly the boys met up with a troop of Hitler Youth from Saxony who sang some Nazi marching songs. One pupil recorded for *"The Gordonian"* in 1937 that,

> *" We couldn't allow this to pass unchallenged, so we responded with a ditty wherein the gentleman and his dog go and mow a meadow, this being our 'piece de resistance'."*

Such was the martial vigour of the pre-war Gordonian ! Involvement in trips abroad has greatly increased over the years and participation in school cruises - latterly on the S.S. Uganda - continued under the supervision of Mr. Marshall and Mr. Jermieson.

In the 1920's and early 30's there appear to have been fewer clubs and societies compared with today. There was for example no longer a College

Gordon's Boys Meet the Hitler Youth 1937

cadet force or associated pipe band. However the 1930's group remember Mr. Kerr Hunter organising an after school club where,

> *"....you could play darts or chess or basketball."*

There was of course a school choir and orchestra and a Dramatic Society. The Society's last performance of *"The Auld Hoose"*, which has been mentioned before, was 1957 but the pupils of the 50's, 60's and 70's speak warmly of the Gilbert and Sullivan productions held every two years. During the 1940's the Literary and Debating Society began and with Dr. Forrest's keen interest quickly attained the high standards of debating and public speaking for which the College is still recognised. Alan McLean (1974-80) remembers not only the fun of participating but also the skills acquired,

> *"....which held me in good stead for later in life."*

The history of the College Cadet Force stretches back to the beginning of the century. During World War 1 Alexander Gray (1912-17) recalls becoming,

> *"...a member of the Cadet Battalion. I volunteered to do a few things, one of which was farm work.....Then went to Inverness with the Cadets and worked in a camp for a week trimming bark off tree stumps. The trees in*

the woods had been cut down to make into short lengths by German prisoners of war...The timbers were then shipped to the battlefields and used to prop up the trenches..."

In 1941 the Air Training Corps was set up and the modern Army Cadet Force dates from 1948. By the 1950's large numbers of boys were participating and Keith Philip (1955-61) says,

" I particularly enjoyed shooting and we had a good shooting team."

The rifle range was situated at the back of the school where the Blackfriars building now is. One of the few groups, by contrast, which has not continued to thrive is the Scouts. The 1930's pupils remember three Scout troops attached to the College but by the 1950's there were two - the 19th and 30th - which met on Friday evenings and were still very popular. Unfortunately as one of the 1950's group explains,

".....they survived well into the 1960's and then the 19th slowly disappeared as numbers in the Scout movement began to wane and gradually the 30th fell into difficulties. They couldn't get leaders and that's why the College scout troops finally ended."

Air Training Corps 1941

Dancing is not an activity which many would associate with the male dominated Gordon's College of old. However not only was it part of the school curriculum, but for many pupils of the 30's, 40's and 50's it was synonymous with the name Madame Murray. Madame Murray joined the College as a part-time teacher of Physical Training and *"Eurythmics"*. She introduced the primary boys to various forms of dance, including tap and highland. Demonstrations of the latter were a common feature of some public occasions. In addition Madame Murray taught ballroom dancing on Saturday evenings at various venues over time, including the Cowdray Hall. Learning such skills had a particularly significant advantage for the boys as Charles Milne (1936-42) points out,

> *"Madame Murray did a tremendous social thing for us, it wasn't just dancing. She introduced us to girls you know - a boys school and getting to Madame's and actually touching and holding a girl and dancing !"*

Madame Murray retired in 1957 and David Milne (1951-62) gives an insight into why,

> *"She retired because of us.....she taught us all to do the sword dance, to be performed on Sports Day...it was so bad that the piper could hardly play for laughing.....all the parents were in absolute hysterics and Madame Murray disappeared out of the side gate never to be seen again !"*

Despite the retiral of Madame Murray the Gordon's boys of later generations still managed to meet up with members of the opposite sex. In the 1960's the Rendezvous Cafe and Boots became favoured meeting places with the Albyn girls. In the 1970's St. Margarets School dancing classes along with Ron's dancing classes in Queens Cross Hall served a similar purpose to Madame Murray's. Happily the tradition of learning to dance in preparation for the senior dances at Christmas has been continued with Mr. Cumming and Miss McNaught, and this is another example of the great tradition of Gordon's staff giving of their time to allow pupils to pursue a huge range of extra - curricular activities.Indeed the blossoming of clubs and societies in the 80's and 90's which many interviewees have referred to, bears witness to this ongoing commitment.

Chapter 6

The end of boarding, girls in the school and other memorable days.

Despite the fact that Gordon's Hospital was originally opened in 1750 as a boarding establishment, it became a day school in 1881. It wasn't until 1937 that boarding was re-established with the opening of Sillerton House in 1937. Occupying numbers 15 and 16 Albyn Place, Sillerton House was later extended as boarding numbers rapidly rose, with the purchase of number 14. Pupils have commented on the high standards of discipline set by the first Housemaster Mr. George Barton who held the post until 1964. However within two years or so of Mr. Barton's appointment World War II broke out. The basement of the house provided an ideal air raid shelter and the boarders helped with *"blacking out"*. The following verse is taken from a poem which appeared in the 1940 edition of *"The Sillertonian"*, a magazine produced by the boarders -

Just now we have the blackout

And screen our window panes,

Just because Old Nasty

Comes and bombs us in his planes

J.C. Walker IIIB

Boarding is re-established at Gordon's - the Opening of Sillerton House 1937

Some boarders didn't see their parents *"for the duration"* and in one or two cases, because of internment by the Japanese, never again. Food rationing was a feature of life at this time and this continued to affect the boarders, like everybody else, into the immediate post - war era. Thus boarders were required to hand in their *"coupons"*. Forbes Young (1952-57) provides a good outline of life at Sillerton House during these years of austerity. Eight to ten younger boys would share a dormitory and sleep in beds with metal springs and horse hair mattresses. Corporal punishment would be administered *" ...with a gym. shoe on the bottom"*. During the week the boarders would walk back from Schoolhill to have lunch at Sillerton House - a tradition which continued until the closure of the house. Homework was completed during *"prep"* time in the evenings after tea. Most boys were involved in sport on Saturday mornings with some free time on Saturday afternoons. Older boys were allowed to go to Madame Murray's between 7-30 and 9-00 on Saturday evening. On Sundays in the 40's, 50's and 60's the boys would attend the morning service at St Nicholas Kirk where dark suits or kilts were worn.

Former pupils, both boarders and non - boarders, have commented on the fact that the Sillerton boys were perceived as *" being different"* although there was a strong and recognisable 'esprit de corps' among the boys - and later girls - of *"the bunk"*, as the boarding house came to be called. Events like the Christmas party, with the dreaded *"party piece"* expected from each boy, helped to foster this sense of community. Being able to play sport, or at least kick a football, does seem to have been an attribute which allowed the boarders to become more easily assimilated into their new surroundings. There were inevitably examples of unhappiness, through home - sickness or occasional bullying, although much of positive value was derived from the experience of boarding. Neil Farquharson (1971 - 77) believes that boarding at Sillerton

"....taught me to be independent and to make up my own mind."

He also records that the surroundings did become rather less severe with the arrival of John and May Dow,

"......it was friendly and we had proper mattresses on the beds."

Housemasters of Sillerton Boarding House 1995
Left to right - Andrew Thorpe (1989-95), John Dow (1974-89), George Barton (1937-64), Howard Smith (1969-73), Iain Brown (1964-69)

In spite of selling off number 14 Albyn Place in order to improve facilities and refurbish the remainder of the house in the late 1980's, boarding numbers dropped steadily. This reflected national trends and even with the intake of girl boarders the decline continued and Sillerton House closed in 1995. However despite the sad demise of boarding, the coming of the girls to the school had opened a new chapter in the story of Gordon's College.

The ending of 239 years of single sex schooling came on 23 August 1989 when the first girls to wear the Gordon's uniform entered the College. A photograph in the *"Press and Journal"* recorded this historic event and some of these girls - now ladies - agreed to talk about their experiences. The reasons for girls coming to the school varied greatly. For those who moved from St. Margarets or Albyn it was a desire for a more *"normal"* co-educational environment which would, at the same time, push them academically. For some of the girls it was part of a family tradition where father was a Gordonian and/or brothers were at Gordon's - the latter meaning that school *"runs"* were much more convenient for mum ! One of the first girls illustrates the the strength of the Gordonian connection despite paternal failings at school,

> *"My dad was academically useless. I think he left when he was fifteen and it was in the days of A,B,C,D and E classes. He was an E boy and I think he was made to feel totally stupid...but he has happy memories of his friends."*

The First Gordon's Girls 1989
Reproduced courtesy of Aberdeen Journals

The large size of the school was what initially impressed the female newcomers. Some of the girls found being so outnumbered by the boys quite intimidating, especially for those like Elizabeth Templeton (1990-94) who was the only girl in a Higher Chemistry set. Also, Jennifer Graham (1991-95) records her surprise,

> *".....when everyone said you had to put your hand up and say 'Sir'. I found that unfriendly."*

Perhaps less surprising was the fact that the girls in S1 and S2 did Technical Drawing along with Metalwork and Woodwork. There was no provision for Home Economics. Facilities for the girls were good, as Esther Krukowski (1989-95) points out,

> *".....you could go for swimming, about six of you in a class with several changing cubicles each!"*

Also there is the suggestion that the girls were favoured in other ways,

> *"Maybe the teachers thought we were so weak we couldn't handle this male -dominated environment.....we were afforded liberties.."*

Of course for the younger girls there was the added advantage of joining a male dominated institution as one records,

> *"I can safely say that 99% of the Sixth Year boys were just tall and gorgeous !"*

The First Founder's Day 1934
Recorded in The Bon-Accord

although she does add with a hint of bitterness,

"When we reached Sixth Year the boys were immature and unattractive!"

For the girls, as for all pupils in the College, the memorable public events in the school calendar have continued to be Prize-giving and Founder's Day. The first Founder's Day took place in 1934 and it was very much a special day. In addition to parading across Schoolhill to St. Nicholas Kirk and listening to the Founder's Day address, the afternoon was taken up with sports at Seafield and a performance of *"The Auld Hoose"* in the evening ! This full day series of events did not continue for very long and pupils were allowed a half day holiday. One pupil of the 1980's offers this minority view of the Founder's Day ceremony,

"I remember having this feeling that it was unique in our school and it was a day to be proud of in a way."

The rather more commonly held view is expressed by a pupil of the 1970's,

"The oration was normally long and thoroughly boring for everyone. The best bit was betting on the length of the speech and getting a half day holiday !"

The Auld Hoose *(a scene from the play)*

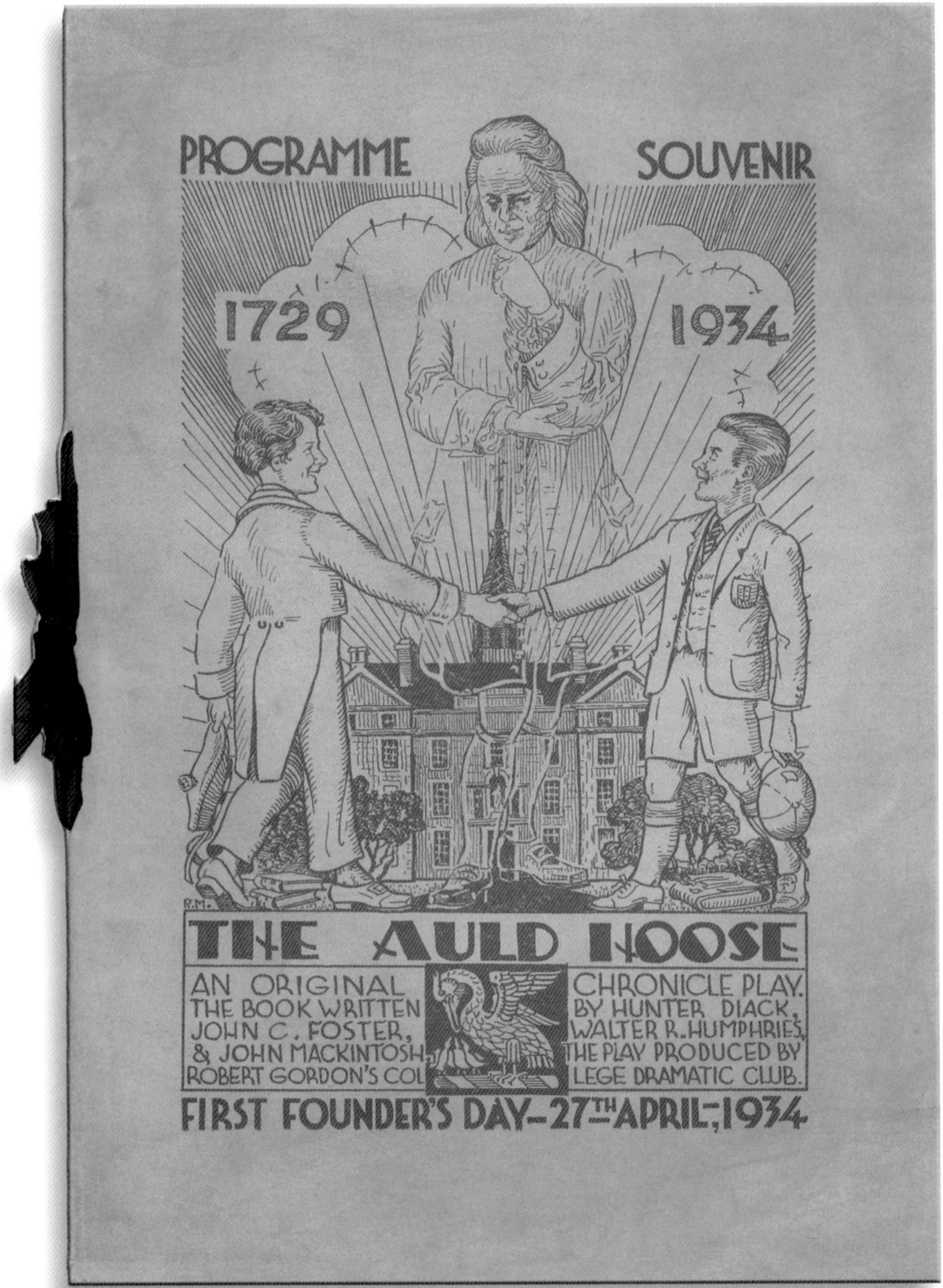

The programme for the first performance of "The Auld Hoose"

Prize-giving in the MacRobert Hall and later the Music Hall was, and continues to be, the most important public event of the school year. For the minority of pupils who receive prizes it is an event which engenders much pride and perhaps some embarrassment. For the remaining majority of pupils the attractions of prize-giving are less obvious, as expressed by Jennifer Black (1990-95),

> *" I just remember it being very, very hot and very long and a lot of clapping."*

However a younger pupil of the 1980's describes a strategy for relieving any boredom,

> *" We used to entertain ourselves by having a contest to see who would start the clapping first and who was the last to clap."*

How sad for innumerable guest speakers who have mistakenly believed that the speed and spontaneity of the applause from the pupils was a reflection on the quality of the speeches !

Finally mention must be made of the old school songs. The Gordonian Song, *"Out from the vaulted gateway..",* was sung by the boys from the mid-1930's having originally been sung as a solo from Scene V of *"The Auld Hoose"* in 1934. In the early 1960's a version in Latin came to be performed and it appeared in the prize-giving programme as late as 1988. With the move to co-education this musical tradition ended. It is perhaps surprising that the majority of the 1990's group expressed sadness at its demise and most supported its revival. In response to their enthusiasm and to further awaken memories of Gordon's College of old, the words of both songs are reproduced below -

School Song

Gordonienses sumus, qui laeti cantamus,
Nos pueri virique Collegiae praeclarae.
Concordia cum magna, voces remittimus
Per terram Scotorum atqu' alienorum

Gordonienses nos, hic omnes hodie,
Maiorum natu memores et Scholae fideles,
Omni nunc arte magistra
Carmen superbum clamemus,
'Gordonienses nos.'

Gordonian Song

Out from the vaulted gateway with the march of eager feet
The lads of the laughing legions fare forth the world to meet
The world to meet and master O Wizardry benign
Omni Nunc Arte Magistra sings in your heart and mine

Chorus -

For we're a' Gordonians here
We're a' Gordonians here
Tho' far and lang the road we gang
We're a' Gordonians here
Tho' far and lang the road we gang
There's ae bield whar we aye belang
The bield we'll aye hold dear

We are the lads of Gordon's
And Gordon's aye we'll be
What'er the fates we follow
What'er the lands we see
On soldier sage or toiler
The olden glamour falls
We're sons to greet a mother
Within these storied walls

Set in yon stately city
O school of memory
All winds of the world are wafting
Our dream thoughts back to thee.
Where aye the turf is green lads
And youth will clarion still
And the morning stars be shining
Above the old Schoolhill